Deserts

KINGFISHER
LONDON & NEW YORK

Distributed in the U.S. and Canada by Macmillan, 175 Fifth Ave., New York, NY 10010

First published as *Kingfisher Young Knowledge: Deserts* in 2005
Additional material produced for Macmillan Children's Books by Discovery Books Ltd.

Library of Congress Cataloging-in-Publication data has been applied for.

ISBN: 978-0-7534-6836-4

Kingfisher books are available for special promotions and premiums. For details contact:
Special Markets Department, Macmillan, 175 Fifth Ave., New York, NY 10010.

For more information, please visit www.kingfisherbooks.com

Printed in China
1 3 5 7 9 8 6 4 2
1TR/0512/UTD/WKT/140MA

Note to readers: the website addresses listed in this book are correct at the time of going to print. However, due to the ever-changing nature of the Internet, website addresses and content can change. Websites can contain links that are unsuitable for children. The publisher cannot be held responsible for changes in website addresses or content or for information obtained through a third party. We strongly advise that Internet searches are supervised by an adult.

Acknowledgments
The publisher would like to thank the following for permission to reproduce their material. Every care has been taken to trace copyright holders. However, if there have been unintentional omissions or failure to trace copyright holders, we apologize and will, if informed, endeavor to make corrections in any future edition.
b = bottom, c = center, l = left, t = top, r = right

Photographs: cover all images courtesy of Shutterstock.com; 1 Getty Imagebank; 2–3 Corbis/Firefly Productions; 4–5 Corbis/Gavriel Jecan; 6–7 Getty Taxi; 8*t* Panoramic Images/Warren Marr; 8*b* Corbis/Dean Conger; 9*t* Corbis/Michael & Patricia Fogden; 9*b* Corbis/Owen Franken; 10–11 Still Pictures/Frans Lemmens; 11*t* Corbis/Peter Johnson; 11*b* Corbis/Peter Johnson; 12–13 Corbis/Peter Lillie; Gallo Images; 12*t* Panoramic Images/Warren Marr; 12*b* Science Photo Library/David Scharf; 14–15 Getty Taxi; 14*b* Getty Imagebank; 15*tr* Corbis/Dewitt Jones; 15*br* Corbis/Martin Harvey; Gallo Images; 16–17 Getty National Geographic; 16*cr* Getty Imagebank; 16*b* NHPA/Darryl Balfour; 17*cl* NHPA/Martin Harvey; 17*r* Corbis; 18–19 Ardea/John Cancalosi; 18 Ardea/Pat Morris; 19 Minden Pictures; 20–21 Corbis; 20*cl* Minden Pictures; 20*b* Frank Lane Picture Agency; 21*tr* Michael & Patricia Fogden; 21*br* NHPA/Daniel Heuclin; 22–23 Getty Imagebank; 22*cr* Corbis/Martin Harvey; Gallo Images; 23*tr* Ardea/Ken Lucas; 24–25 Getty Photographer's Choice; 25*tr* Corbis/Hans Georg Roth; 26–27 Still Pictures; 27*tr* Corbis/Richard Powers; 28–29 Still Pictures; 29*tr* Corbis/Derek Trask; 30–31 Still Pictures; 30*b* Corbis/Janet Jarman; 31*tr* Science Photo Library/Peter Ryan; 32–33 Corbis/K. M. Westermann; 32*bl* Getty Imagebank; 33*br* Getty Imagebank; 34–35 Getty Stone; 34*cl* Corbis; 35*t* Corbis/Carl & Ann Purcell; 35*c* Corbis/Paul A. Souders; 36–37 Corbis/Sergio Pitamitz; 36*b* Getty Stone; 37*br* Corbis/Hughes Martin; 38–39 Science Photo Library/Martin Bond; 38*b* British Museum; 39*t* Getty National Geographic; 39*b* Corbis/James L. Amos; 40–41 Alamy/Steve Bloom; 41*t* Getty National Geographic; 48*l* Shutterstock/Styve Reineck; 48*r* Shutterstock/Curioso; 49 Shutterstock/Patrick Poendi; 52*t* Shutterstock/Hagit Berkovich; 52*b* Joao Virissimo; 53 Shutterstock/James M. Phelps, Jr.; 56 Shutterstock/Songquan Deng

Commissioned artwork on page 7 by Encompass Graphics
Commissioned photography on pages 42–47 by Andy Crawford
Thank you to models Lewis Manu and Rebecca Roper

discover science

Deserts

Nicola Davies

KINGFISHER
NEW YORK

Contents

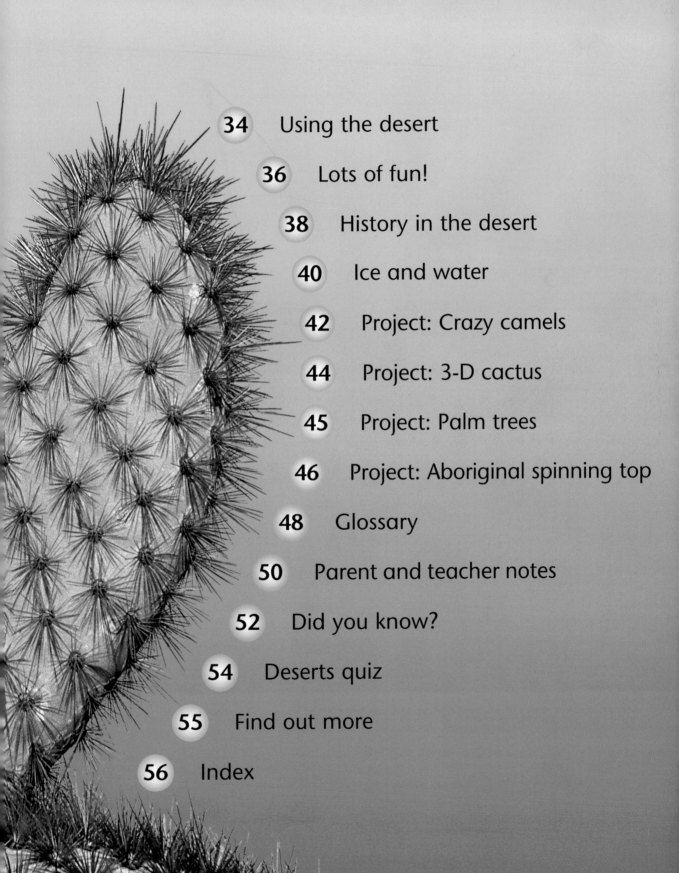

What is a desert?

A desert is a place where it almost never rains. This makes deserts the driest places on Earth and the hardest in which to live.

All around the world

Almost one fourth of the land on our planet is covered in deserts. Wherever there is a desert, there are animals and plants that have found a way to survive the harsh, dry conditions.

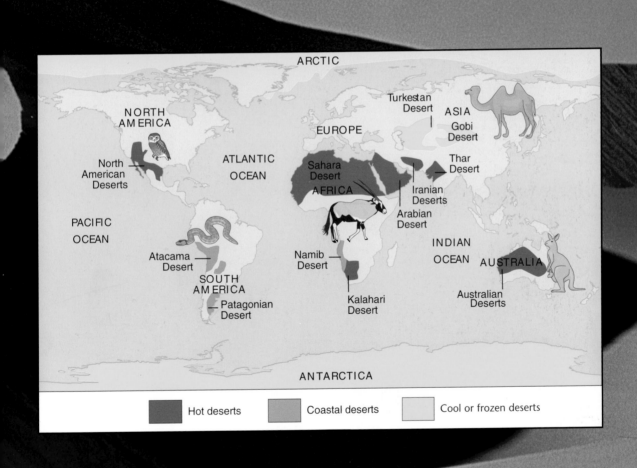

ARCTIC

NORTH AMERICA

North American Deserts

ATLANTIC OCEAN

PACIFIC OCEAN

Atacama Desert

SOUTH AMERICA

Patagonian Desert

EUROPE

Turkestan Desert

Sahara Desert

AFRICA

Namib Desert

Kalahari Desert

ASIA

Gobi Desert

Thar Desert

Iranian Deserts

Arabian Desert

INDIAN OCEAN

AUSTRALIA

Australian Deserts

ANTARCTICA

Hot deserts | Coastal deserts | Cool or frozen deserts

Looking different

Not all deserts are hot and sandy. They can be pebbly, cool, rocky, mountainous, or even a mixture of these. Every desert is unique.

Hot Mojave

The Mojave Desert in North America was once the bottom of a lake. Now, it is a huge plain covered in cracked, dried mud and pebbles.

Cool Gobi

In Mongolia's Gobi Desert, the wind always blows from the same direction. This shapes the sand dunes and pushes them forwards.

Hot Sahara

These rocks are found in mountains that are part of the Sahara. They are so high that they are covered in frost in the winter.

Coastal desert

Fog blows in from the ocean next to the Namib Desert. This brings water to some of the highest sand dunes in the world.

Wild weather

Desert weather is extreme. Clear blue skies mean that deserts are almost always sunny and hot during the day. But at night, it is a very different story.

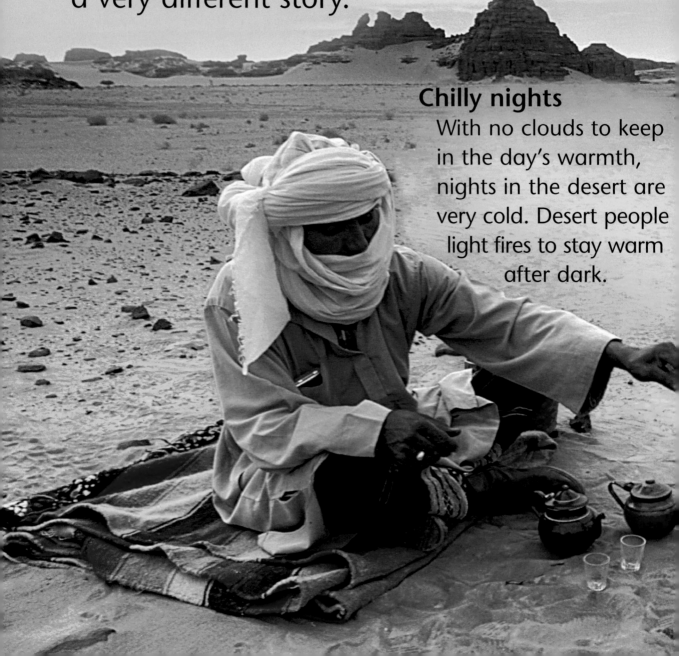

Chilly nights

With no clouds to keep in the day's warmth, nights in the desert are very cold. Desert people light fires to stay warm after dark.

Roasting days

It may be freezing at midnight, but by noon in the desert it is very hot. Animals, such as these springbok, have to shelter from the sun.

Staying warm . . . and cool

Desert squirrels use their bushy tail to help them cope with the extreme weather. In the cold night, the tail is like a fluffy blanket. But during the hot day, it is a perfect sunshade.

Whistling wind

Deserts are so windy that almost every one has a wind with its own special name. For example, the wind in Algeria is called the Khamsin, and in North America it is called the Chubaseos.

Dusty gusts

Sometimes, desert winds pick up sand and dust and blow them around in storms that can last for days. This makes it difficult to see and even to breathe.

Sandy sculpture

Gusts full of sand and dust slowly wear away rocks. Over thousands of years, the rocks are transformed into strange shapes, such as these amazing formations in the Mojave Desert.

Smoothest sand

Desert winds rub sand grains together. This makes the grains smooth and round.

Desert rain

Rain in the desert is very rare. So when there are showers, desert plants and animals have to make the most of them.

Stormy weather

Heavy rain often follows thunder and lightning. In some deserts, storms bring rain every year, but other deserts can stay dry for more than ten years.

Be quick!

As soon as it rains, frogs lay their eggs in rainwater pools. Their tadpoles must grow quickly and change into frogs before the pools dry out.

Beautiful blooms

Desert plants flower after it rains, so the whole desert looks like a carpet of blossoms. When the flowers dry out and die they leave seeds behind. These seeds sprout the next time it rains.

Prickly plants

Desert plants are tough. They have thicker skins, smaller leaves, and more spines than other plants. This stops the heat from drying them out, and keeps hungry animals away.

Drop that leaf!
Creosote bushes from North America lose their leaves when it is dry—but when it rains, they grow them again.

The Namib's dew collector
Leaves of the strange-looking welwitschia plant bend over onto the ground. Fog and dew stick to the leaves, making droplets of water that run down to the roots.

Lots of spikes

Saguaro cacti from Arizona have no leaves. Instead, they store water in their huge stems. These stems are protected by thick skin and many prickly spikes.

Hide-and-seek!

Only the tops of the stone plant's two fat leaves peek above the ground's surface. The plant hides from the sun and drying winds until it rains. Only then is it able to flower.

Desert fliers

Flight makes desert life easier for birds because they can travel long distances to find food and water. But they still have to cope with the hot days and cold nights.

Burrow nester

The tiny elf owl makes use of the cool twilight to hunt for small mammals, reptiles, and insects. It nests under the ground, where its eggs are protected from the fierce heat that could easily cook them in their shells.

Cactus surgeons

Woodpeckers make holes in the
rotten or broken stems of giant
saguaro cacti. The birds nest in
the cool holes and peck away
any sick parts of a cactus. This
stops disease from spreading to
the whole plant.

Roadrunner stretches

Desert roadrunners warm up
after the cold desert night by
lifting their neck feathers and
letting the sun shine on a patch
of special skin. This skin soaks
up heat and keeps them warm.

Little creatures

Insects, reptiles, and rodents thrive in the desert because they do not need much water. They can also hide from the heat, wind, or cold in burrows.

Honey bellies

Desert honey ants store precious water and nectar in their blown-up bellies. This supply helps the ant colony survive when there is no food or water.

Sleep by night

Reptiles such as this chuckwalla stay under the ground in the cold of night. When morning comes, they lie in the sun to warm up.

Fog bathers

Darkling beetles find something to drink by trapping the droplets of water from fog on their legs and tipping the water toward their mouths.

Sleep by day

Animals such as this small gerbil are warm-blooded. They search for food in the cold night, but during the day, they hide in underground burrows to stay cool.

Mighty mammals

Large mammals that live in deserts cannot shelter from the sun in burrows like their smaller relatives do. They must find other ways to beat the heat.

Dig out to chill out
To cool their bellies, kangaroo scrape away at the hot surface sand and lie down on the colder sand underneath.

Color-coded

Fennec foxes' pale fur helps reflect the heat and keep them cool—just like a white T-shirt keeps you cool on a hot summer day.

Camel cooler

At night, camels' bodies become very cold. So although the sun warms them all day, they are never too hot.

Pools of water

Rivers flowing through a desert or bubbling up from under the ground can bring water all year long to deserts. A place where this happens is called an oasis.

Green and growing

Oases are bustling with life. Tall trees, such as palms, and many types of animals can live in oases because there is plenty of water.

Walking to water

Oases are very important to desert peoples and their animals. They may travel hundreds of miles to find water at a familiar oasis—even if the water is at the bottom of a well.

Desert dwellers

People have lived in deserts for thousands of years. They have learned all sorts of ways to cope with the difficulties of desert life.

People who wander
Many desert people are nomads. They live in tents and move around to find fresh water and grazing sites for their animals.

Water carriers
Women in India's Thar Desert carry water from faraway wells in large jars that they balance on their heads.

Growing deserts

Deserts are important and beautiful wild places. But they are expanding unnaturally because of some of the things that humans do. Every year, growing deserts swallow up valuable grassland, farmland, and forests.

Too much munching

Where people let their animals eat all of the plants, the sun and wind can hit the bare ground. This turns the soil into dust and makes it difficult to regrow plants.

Bad gas!

Cars, airplanes, and factories emit gases that make the weather hotter. This is called global warming. It is worse in places that are already hot and dry, so it makes deserts grow.

Making deserts green

People can help stop deserts from expanding by planting trees and grass to protect the soil. Irrigating the desert helps keep plants alive.

Rain saving

Saving rainwater with dams means that there will be water for crops. This woman is harvesting food in what was once a desert.

Magic water

Usually, water runs through sand and is lost. Adding flakes of special plastic to the water helps soil hold onto it and helps plants grow.

Green . . . and greener

Growing plants also helps cool the ground and the air above. This means that the soil stays moist and the desert cannot expand.

Cities in the desert

There are cities in deserts all over the world. But cities with millions of people use a lot of water—and that is a big problem in any desert.

Bright lights, big city
Las Vegas, located in a desert in Nevada, is so big that it uses water from hundreds of miles away. This lack of water threatens both the wildlife and farmland with drought.

Green, green city

Abu Dhabi, on the coast of the United Arab Emirates, uses fresh water from the ocean by taking out the salt! This means that there is enough water to create green spaces that keep the city cool.

Ways to save water

Kerzaz, an ancient city in the Sahara Desert, needs much less water than a modern town. People there carefully use water and know that every drop is precious.

Using the **desert**

Deserts may look empty, but they have hidden treasures. They also give us the space to do things that are dangerous anywhere else.

Deadly testing

The world's deadliest weapons— nuclear bombs—were tested in deserts where they could not kill anyone. But these bombs left the land poisoned for many years after testing.

Hidden energy

Petroleum is found under some deserts. It is pumped and carried to cities and other countries in huge pipes like this one.

Underground jewels

Opals were formed
millions of years ago
when water drained
from rocks under
the ground. This
ground is now the
Australian deserts,
and almost all of
the world's opals
are mined there!

Lots of fun!

Sunny blue skies and beautiful scenery make deserts great places to relax, but some people prefer a little more action

Sandboarding

You can go down a sand dune the same way that you can slide down a snowy slope. You can even surf a dune like a big wave in the ocean!

Desert racer

Dune buggies can climb steep dunes and zoom around the desert without getting stuck in the sand. They are a lot of fun, but their tires can damage desert plants.

Comfortable climbing

Rock formations found in deserts are warm and dry. This makes them easier to climb than mountains where the weather is cold, wet, and icy.

History in the desert

We can learn about the past in deserts because the hot, dry air preserves dead bodies. Sand covers the dried remains of people, plants, and animals and, because few people live in deserts, the remains can lie undisturbed for a long time.

Mummies from long ago

Bodies buried in deserts dry out very quickly, so skin, hair, and clothes can last for thousands of years. Preserved dead bodies—called mummies— found in deserts show us how people looked and dressed a long time ago.

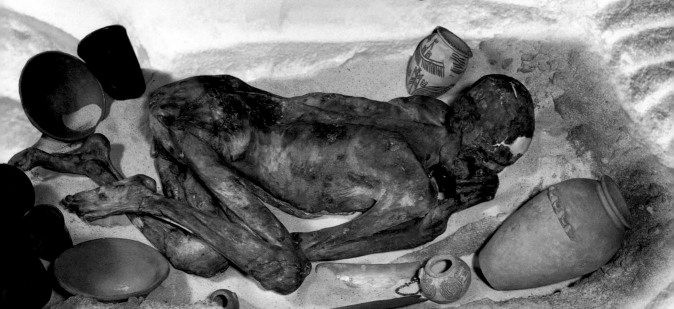

Rock art

Thousands of years ago, people painted pictures on rocks in the Namib. They show that the desert used to be grassland bustling with people and animals.

Desert dinos

Some of the world's most exciting dinosaur fossils have been found in deserts. The dry winds wear away rocks and bring fossil bones close to the surface.

Ice and water

Not all deserts are hot and dusty—some are found in the coldest parts of the world! The word "desert" can also be used to describe places where conditions are simply too tough for life to survive.

Lifeless blue

There can be no life in the ocean without phytoplankton. In places where plankton does not grow, the ocean can be a wet and salty desert.

Icy deserts

Some parts of the Arctic receive less rain than Africa's Sahara Desert. These areas are too cold and dry for anything to grow. Polar bears survive by walking to the ocean to catch seals.

Crazy camels

Salt train

Selling salt is a very important way for desert people to make money. Loads of salt are carried across the desert on camels.

camel template

You will need:

- Brown card stock
- Tracing paper
- Pencil
- Scissors
- Permanent marker
- Foil candy wrappers
- Glue
- Gold or silver thread

1

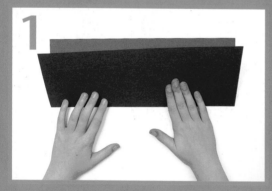

Fold the brown card stock in half. Put the piece of tracing paper over the camel template and trace over the camel shape.

2

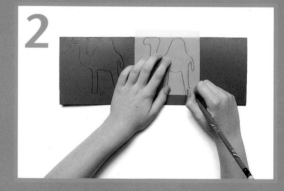

Put the traced template onto the card stock so that the camel's hump is on the fold. Trace the camel onto the card stock three times to make three camels.

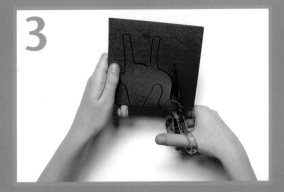

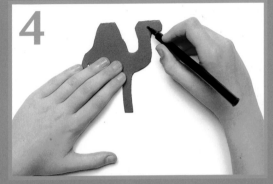

Using the scissors, carefully cut out the three camel shapes. Make sure you do not cut through the humps at the fold.

Holding a camel firmly with one hand, use the permanent marker to draw the eyes and noses on each camel.

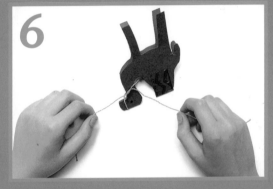

Smooth out three different foil candy wrappers. Glue them onto the middle of the camels' backs. You may need to cut the wrappers if they are too long.

To make the camels' bridles, tie thread around the camels' necks. Use the thread to join the camels together so that they are ready to carry salt across the desert.

3-D cactus

Slit and slide!

A saguaro cactus can be more than 30 ft. (10m) tall and have five arms. Some saguaro are more than 200 years old!

You will need:
- Pencil
- Tracing paper
- Thick green card stock
- Scissors

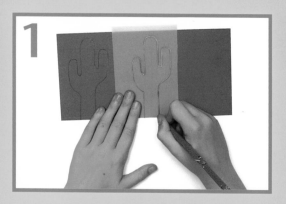

Trace the cactus template onto tracing paper. Then, use the template to trace two cacti onto the green card.

slit 1 (step 2)

cactus template

slit 2 (step 3)

Cut out the two cactus shapes. Following the template, use the scissors to cut a slit halfway down one cactus.

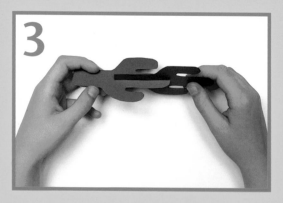

Cut a slit halfway up the second cactus. Slide the first cactus into the second. If you want, decorate the cactus with green glitter.

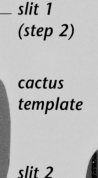

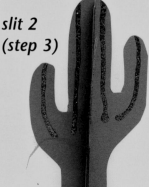

Palm trees

Bend and shape it!

Palm trees are often found at oases in the Sahara. Desert peoples rest in the shade of palms when it is hot.

You will need:
- 2 strips of brown card stock
- Glue
- Green card stock
- Double-sided tape
- Shoebox lid
- Sand

To make the palm's trunk, glue the brown card stock to make an "L" shape. Fold the card stock over itself to make accordion folds.

To make the palm's leaves, cut the green card stock into five curved strips. Fold each strip like a fan and it will spring open.

Fill a shoebox lid with sand and put the camels, 3-D cactus, and palm tree in the lid to create your own desert landscape.

Cut a small piece of double-sided tape and stick it in the middle of the palm's trunk. Stick each of the five leaves onto the trunk.

Aboriginal spinning top

Smart symbols

The Aboriginal people of Australia's deserts painted symbols on rocks. Now, artists use these symbols to paint modern art.

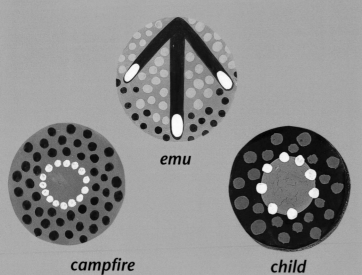

emu

campfire

child

You will need:

- Pencil
- Mug
- Cup
- Small plate
- Cardboard
- Scissors
- Paints
- Paintbrush
- Modelling clay
- Compass
- Chopstick

1

To make five disks, trace on the cardboard around the mug twice, the cup twice, and the small plate once. Carefully cut out each disk.

2

Paint the disks using orange or yellow paints—if you want, each circle can be a different color. Leave the disks to dry thoroughly.

Following the examples on page 46, paint one side of each disk with a different Aboriginal symbol. When the paint is dry, turn each disk over and paint the same symbol on the other side.

Place a ball of modeling clay under the middle of each disk. Use the point of the compass to pierce a hole in the middle of each disk.

When all five disks are on the chopstick, stand the top upright and spin it around.

To put the disks on the chopstick, start with one of the disks from the cup and the mug, then the disk from the plate, and the last two from the mug and cup. The disks should be evenly spaced.

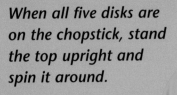

Glossary

burrow—hole or tunnel under the ground

bustling—busy

conditions—how things are around you

dew—small drops of water that form at night on grass and plants

drought—a long period of time when there is no water

emit—to give off

expanding—getting bigger

extreme weather—very hot or cold, dry or wet, or windy weather

fog—a low cloud of tiny drops of water

formation—a pattern

fossil—the remains of an ancient animal or plant turned to rock

global warming—an increase in the world's overall temperature, thought to be caused by pollution

gust—a sudden blast of wind

irrigating—watering big areas such as whole fields

mammal—a warm-blooded animal that feeds its young on milk produced by the mother

moist—damp

nomad—a person who moves from place to place, taking their home with them

oasis—a place in a desert where there is water

petroleum—the oil used to make fuel for vehicles, to generate electricity, and to make many plastics

phytoplankton—the tiny floating plants found in oceans and seas

plain—a huge flat area of land

rare—when something does not happen very often

reflect—to bounce back

survive—to stay alive

tadpole—a young frog or toad

transform—to change

twilight—when it is not dark or light, at dawn and at dusk

warm-blooded—describes animals that have bodies that can make their own heat

well—a deep hole in the ground with water at the bottom

The content of this book will be useful to help teach and reinforce various elements of the science and language arts curricula in the elementary grades. It also provides opportunities for crosscurricular lessons in geography and art.

Extension activities

Writing and oral language
Select a desert animal and write a short report highlighting the adaptations that enable it to live in desert conditions. Share your information in a short presentation.

Creative writing
Look at the picture of the oasis on pp. 24–25. Imagine that you are in the group of people arriving at the oasis. Where have you been? Where are you going? Write a short story describing your adventures crossing the desert.

Using graphic organizers
Use a Venn diagram to show the similarities and differences between a hot desert and an icy desert.

Science
The study of deserts relates to scientific themes of ecosystems, adaptations, Earth's structures and formation, weather and climate, and interaction with the environment. Some specific links to science curriculum include climate change (pp. 28–29); conservation (pp. 28–33); Earth's history (pp. 38–39); fossils (pp. 38–39); natural resources (pp. 34–35); predator-prey relationships (p. 18); and weathering and erosion (pp. 12–13).

Crosscurricular links
1) Art: Research to find out about Navajo sand painting, and create a picture of your own. Use naturally colored sand or make your own by rubbing small amounts of sand with colored chalk. To make a permanent sand painting, create a pattern of white glue before you add each color. Let the glue dry before adding another color.

2) Geography: Beginning with the map on p. 7, go through the book and list all the deserts mentioned.

Locate each desert on a world map and add the country and continent to your list.

Using the projects
Children can do these projects at home. Here are some ideas for extending them:

Pages 42–43: Camels are just one of the desert animals mentioned in this book. Select a different desert animal (it doesn't have to be a mammal) and create a stand-up model similar to the camel on these pages.

Pages 44–45: Other desert plants with unusual structures include Joshua trees, ocotillos, barrel cacti, beavertail cacti, and mesquites. Research to find out about one or more of these and design a model similar to the others in the activity. You might need to use a larger box lid for a landscape to display your collection of desert plants and animals.

Pages 46–47: What other designs could you use to make a top? Many different cultural groups of Native Americans made, and still make, their homes in the deserts of the Southwest. Research to find distinctive art forms of peoples such as the Hopi, Apache, and Navajo, then create other spinning top designs. Compare the new designs with the Aboriginal symbols.

Did you know?

- More than one billion people—one sixth of Earth's population—actually live in desert regions.

- When captured, the tiny elf owl plays dead until all danger has passed.

- Camels store fat, not water, in their humps. Baby camels are born without humps because the layer of fat doesn't develop until they eat solid food.

- A place that receives less than 10 inches (25 centimeters) of rain in a year is considered a desert.

- The Joshua tree is found only in the Mojave Desert and relies on one kind of moth for pollination.

- The fennec fox's ears are 6 in. (15cm) long. They help the fox radiate body heat and stay cool in the desert heat.

- Twenty percent of Earth's land surface is made up of deserts.

- Desert tortoises spend more than 95 percent of their lives in underground burrows. This is because the ground temperature outside can reach more than 140°F (60°C).

- The Tuareg people live in the Sahara Desert and are sometimes known as the "blue people" because of the color of their traditional blue dress.

- Camels can last up to one week without water and then may drink up to 38 gal. (145L) at one time.

- The Sahara Desert is the second-largest desert in the world after Antarctica, but it is the largest hot desert in the world.

- When full, a saguaro cactus stem can store up to 5.5 tons of water, which is enough for it to survive many months of drought.

- Roadrunners can reach speeds of up to 17 miles (27km) per hour. They are so fast that they can catch and eat rattlesnakes.

- Camels have hairy ears to stop sand from entering them during sandstorms. They can also close their nostrils and have two layers of eyelashes to help protect themselves when it is windy.

- Elf owls don't make any noise as they approach their prey. This is called "silent flight."

- The Mojave Desert spans four American states—Arizona, California, Nevada, and Utah.

Deserts quiz

The answers to these questions can all be found by looking back through the book. See how many you get right. You can check your answers on page 56.

1) Where does the elf owl make its nest?
   A—In a tree
   B—In a cactus
   C—Under the ground

2) How does the roadrunner warm up?
   A—It runs very fast.
   B—It lifts the feathers on its neck for the sun to heat up a special patch of skin.
   C—It lies in the morning sun.

3) What does the saguaro cactus store in its stems?
   A—Water
   B—Nothing
   C—Ice

4) Where do darkling beetles find a drink?
   A—From the leaves of desert plants
   B—They trap water from dew on their legs and slide it into their mouths.
   C—From the surface of rocks

5) What do desert honey ants store in their bellies?
   A—Honey
   B—Water and nectar
   C—Water

6) What is the name given to people who live in the desert and move from place to place?
   A—Herders
   B—Shepherds
   C—Nomads

7) How do kangaroos stay cool?
   A—They go for a swim.
   B—They hop into the shade.
   C—They dig a hole in the hot sand and lie on the cool sand underneath.

8) What is an area of water in the desert called?
   A—An oasis
   B—A river
   C—A puddle

9) Where does the city Abu Dhabi gets its water from?
   A—From rain
   B—From the ocean
   C—From wells deep under the ground

10) Where in the world are most opals mined?
   A—North America
   B—Europe
   C—Australia

11) What is the name given to bodies that are preserved and found in the desert?
   A—Mummies
   B—Corpses
   C—Dummies

12) How are people trying to stop deserts from expanding?
   A—By letting animals eat all of the plants
   B—By planting new trees and plants and saving rainwater
   C—By increasing global warming

Find out more

Books to read
Deserts and Semi-deserts by Michael
    Allaby, Robert Anderson & Ian
    Crofton, Raintree, 2010
*I Wonder Why the Sahara is Cold at Night:
    And Other Questions About Deserts* by
    Jackie Gaff, Kingfisher, 2002
Life Cycles: Desert by Sean Callery,
    Kingfisher, 2012
*The Cat in the Hat Knows a Lot About
    That!: Why Oh Why are Deserts Dry?* by
    Tish Rabe, Bantam Children, 2011
This is a Desert (Readlings) by Gina Cline
    & Trace Taylor, ARC Press, 2011

Places to visit
Arizona-Sonora Desert Museum
www.desertmuseum.org
Visit this great educational museum to
learn all about the Sonoran desert and
the animals, plants, and peoples that
live there. View the Running Wild
demonstration to see some of the
natural behavior of the desert animals,
experience the work of the animal keepers
on the walking tours, and get active on
the butterfly and bird walks, too.

Lincoln Park Zoo, Chicago, Illinois
www.lpzoo.org
Visit this amazing zoo and you can see
a fennec fox, a Kenyan sand boa, and
some new arrivals, including a young
male Bactrian camel. You can also
hop aboard the Express Train or the
Endangered Species Carousel, which
features carvings of some of the rare
and endangered species that you can
visit at the zoo.

Phoenix Zoo, Phoenix, Arizona
www.phoenixzoo.org
There is so much to do at this fantastic
zoo—take a Wild Walk and find out all
about the zoo's animals, ride on the
Safari Train, and stop by at the Stingray
Bay to feed and pet the stingrays. You
can even have your picture taken when
you go on a camel ride.

Websites
www.desertanimals.net
Visit this fantastic website to find out
all about animals that live in the desert.
Find out which desert each animal
lives in and what they eat, as well as
other interesting facts.

*www.desertmuseum.org/kids/oz/
long-fact-sheets*
Check out this site to find some great
fact sheets on Sonoran desert animals,
plants, and peoples. You can find out
about the habitat, diet, predators, and
range of each animal and some extra
fun facts, too.

*http://environment.nationalgeographic.com/
environment/habitats/desert-profile/*
Check out this website to find out all
about deserts. You can also view
photos of some of the desert's most well-
adapted animals and see how global
warming is affecting these habitats.

Deserts quiz answers

1) C	7) C
2) B	8) A
3) A	9) B
4) B	10) C
5) B	11) A
6) C	12) B